PIONEER GARDENS

AT BLACK CREEK PIONEER VILLAGE

EUSTELLA LANGDON

Holt, Rinehart and Winston of Canada, Ltd.
Toronto   Montreal

Distributed in the United States of America by Winston Press, Minneapolis.

TO JOHN
with love

Distribution in the United States of America by
Winston Press,
25 Groveland Terrace,
Minneapolis, Minnesota 55403.

2   3   4   5   76   75   74   73

TABLE OF CONTENTS

4

ACKNOWLEDGEMENTS

I am indebted to many people for their help in writing this book. In particular I should like to express my gratitude to Mrs. John Kinsey of The Garden Club of Toronto, Convener of the Black Creek Pioneer Village Project; to Dr. Elizabeth Chant Robertson of The Hospital for Sick Children, Toronto; and to Miss Dorothy Burke.

For their assistance in various ways I am most grateful to the following: Miss Edith Firth, Associate Head, Metropolitan Toronto Central Library; Mrs. Antony McGrath, Head, Canadian History and Manuscripts Section, Metropolitan Toronto Central Library; Miss Marion Brown, Head, Department of Rare Books and Special Collections, University of Toronto Library, and Mr. Herbert C. Scholler, Associate Librarian (Reader Services); the late Verschoyle Benson Blake, Department of Public Records and Archives, Toronto; Mrs. J. H. Baillie; Mr. H. C. Cross; and Mrs. J. W. Beattie; Dr. J. H. Soper, Chief of Botany Division, National Museum of Natural Sciences, Ottawa; Mrs. J. R. M. Wilson; Professor J. E. Cruise and Leila Gad, Vascular Plant Herbarium, and Dr. Roy Cain, Cryptogamic Herbarium, Department of Botany, University of Toronto.

For various documents generously lent to me, I thank the following: Mr. and Mrs. John C. Burns; Mrs. E. John B. How; Miss Cicely Blackstock; The Hon. Chief Justice Dalton Wells; Mrs. Percy C. Band; Mrs. Curtiss W. Reed; and Miss Judith McErvel of the Archives of Eaton's of Canada.

Finally, I extend sincere thanks to Mr. Russell Cooper, Administrator of Historical Sites, Metropolitan Toronto and Region Conservation Authority, and to the staff at Black Creek Pioneer Village.

EUSTELLA LANGDON

TORONTO NURSERIES.

LESLIE P.O., *19 Nor.* 1874

GEO. LESLIE & SONS,
PROPRIETORS.

Wholesale Prices to *M. A. James*

Enfield P.O., for *Spring* of 1875

NOTE—In filling orders at the prices annexed, we reserve the right of selecting the varieties, but will consult the wishes of customers as far as our Stock will admit.

FRUIT DEPARTMENT.	Cts Each
STANDARD APPLES—5 to 7 feet......	14
HALF " " —4 to 6 feet......	12½
DWARF " —2 and 3 years ...	20
CRAB " —5 to 7 feet	15
STANDARD PEARS—5 to 6 feet....	35
DWARF " —2 and 3 years....	25
CHERRIES, Standard and Dwarf—2 and 3 years.......	"
PLUMS, Standard and Dwarf—2 and 3 years	35
GRAPES—2 years	
Chinton	10
Concord..........	15
Delaware	20
Hartford	15
Iona	"
Salem......	30
Allen's Hybrid	30
Eumelan	35
Rogers' Hybrids (leading numb's)	30
GOOSEBERRIES—English varieties, imp..	12½
" Houghton's Seedling...	8
CURRANTS—Black Naples...........	
" Red Cherry, London Red, and White Grape	5
RASPBERRIES—Orange, Red and Black...	5
BLACKBERRIES—Wilson's & Kittatinny	6
ASPARAGUS ROOTS—2 years, per 100...	75
RHUBARB " —Cahoon's, Myatt's, and Victoria	10
STRAWBERRY PLANTS—Wilson, Triumph, &c.	1
SEA KALE ....per dozen...	50

ORNAMENTAL DEPARTMENT.	Cts Each
ACACIA—common, 5 to 6 feet.........	20
ASH—European, 6 to 7 feet.........	25
BIRCH—European, 4 to 5 feet.........	20
ELM—Scotch, 5 to 6 feet	25
HORSE CHESTNUT—5 to 6 feet	30
" —6 to 8 feet	
LARCH—European, 3 to 4 feet......	20
LINDEN—European, 5 to 6 feet	25
MOUNTAIN ASH—5 to 6 feet	20
MAPLE,—Silver 5 to 6 feet......	"
" —Norway 5 to 6 feet......	25
POPLAR—Lombardy, 5 to 7 feet......	15
" —Balsam 5 to 7 feet......	"
" —Silver leaved, 5 to 7 feet......	"
SYCAMORE—English, 5 to 6 feet......	30
THORNS—Flowering, of sorts, 3 to 4 feet	25
WILLOW—Rosemary, 4 to 5 feet......	50

WEEPING TREES.

	Cts Each
ASH—European, ...	50
BIRCH—Cutleaved, 3 to 4 feet.........	75
MOUNTAIN ASH, ...	60
POPLAR—Grandidentata	50
WILLOW—Kilmarnock	60
" —New American	50
" —Babylonica, 5 to 7 feet......	20

CLIMBING SHRUBS.

	Cts Each
CLEMATIS GRAVIOLINS.............	20
BEGONIA—Trumpet Flower	
HONEYSUCKLE—3 kinds	
VIRGINIA CREEPER.	

HOW IT ALL BEGAN

The household garden was once a vital part of every homestead. This book tells about plants grown by pioneers in southern Ontario gardens before 1867; more specifically it deals with plants to be found in the gardens of Black Creek Pioneer Village. As we draw attention to the unfamiliar in familiar plants and emphasize the contribution that plants have made to our early history, we hope to make the gardens of the past more real to those who visit pioneer villages.

To find a *growing* pioneer village within the boundaries of a great modern city is surprising. But in Metropolitan Toronto a village has been created to show the people of today what an early settlement was like, thus deepening our understanding of North America's early social history through buildings, their surroundings and vegetation. Black Creek Pioneer Village represents a typical crossroads settlement, with authentic buildings, five on their original sites and others brought in from nearby towns and hamlets. To assist The Metropolitan Toronto and Region Conservation Authority in carrying out the project, The Garden Club of Toronto volunteered to contribute time and money to plant the gardens, so that visitors to the Village would find the plants that travellers in the early 1800's would have seen in a quiet Upper Canada agricultural community.

A study group of The Garden Club undertook to do research on suitable flower and vegetable gardens. Since no books were available that dealt specifically with pioneer garden plants, the group spent many months researching archives, early advertisements and nursery lists, private papers and diaries. Every known source of information about gardens of those times was tracked down and filed. As a result there is now a clear record of authentic plants of this period.

The gardens have been planned with much thought to the era in which each dwelling was built and to the occupation of the original owners, so that they resemble closely those of the early days. What did the settlers plant in their gardens? Why did they choose to plant what they did? Were their gardens laid out as ours are today?

The answers are to be found in letters and

diaries; in reports of travellers; in bills, receipts, and merchants' accounts; and in many books that record the daily happenings in the pioneer settlements of Upper Canada. Broadsides, which advertised nursery stock, are gold mines of information, as are advertisements in early newspapers. Notebooks and diaries hold important clues to the vegetables and herbs the settlers grew and to the fruit trees they planted; even varieties are sometimes named. Their diaries record the plants for keeping moths at bay, and for keeping ants, flies, and vermin out of the cabins and the food, and still other plants that were used for making dyes to colour wool, to tint hair or to give a healthy glow to sallow cheeks, and to make ink for writing letters 'home'.

Perhaps the most extensive lists of plants grown in the settlers' gardens are found in eighteenth- and nineteenth-century books offering home cures, and in settlers' notebooks describing simple folk remedies. From choice as well as from economic necessity, most of the settlers preferred to rely on simple plant medicines administered by their women.

The plants to be found growing in Black Creek Pioneer Village and in the fields and along roadsides within the Village boundaries are the plants the Upper Canada settlers grew or gathered in the wilds for food, medicine, and many other household uses.

Even in a garden under consistent excellent care, however, nothing remains the same. Over a period of years, gardens and plants change. Varieties naturally interbreed, and may later appear in different forms, so that genuinely old horticultural varieties can no longer be purchased. Therefore, identical duplication of early gardens is impossible. However, seeds, roots and cuttings of plants that were growing in southern Ontario gardens before 1867 have been collected from gardens where they have been growing for more than a hundred years. Consequently, many plants in the Black Creek Village gardens are true descendants of pioneer varieties.

When you visit a re-created pioneer village to study its historic buildings and their furnishings, it is hoped that the information given here will help you to sense the air of bygone days that fills the village streets, and to enjoy its lovely trees and colourful gardens.

Patina Kinsey, *Project Convener*
Eustella Langdon, *Author*

THE BEGINNING

" . . . I and my family are still taking well with this country, and I really do bless God, every day I rise, that He was ever pleased in the course of His Providence to send me and my family to this place."

—James Dobbie writing to his father in Glasgow, Scotland, from Upper Canada, April 24, 1826. From *Third Report on Emigration from the United Kingdom, June 1827*.

When our forefathers settled in the forests of Upper Canada, their first task, after building crude log shelters, was to prepare the land for the seeds and roots which they had brought with them or which they had received from the Government of Upper Canada. These seeds were as important to them as their tools and household belongings.

The house or yard gardens were what we today would call kitchen gardens, and wherever possible they were placed on a slight southern slope, where it would be possible to work the land earlier in the spring. Here would be good drainage, and early frost would flow past the garden in the fall.

Above: The Shanty in the Bush. *From a series of photo-lithographs, "Three Views in the Life of a Canadian Farmer." Artist unknown. Printed in "The British Farmers and Farm Labourers Guide to Ontario, the Premier Province of the Dominion of Canada," by C. Blackett Robinson, Toronto, 1880.*

Public Archives of Canada, Ottawa

Left: In the 1840's Half Way House was built in Scarborough and served as a stagecoach stop on the Kingston-Toronto run. It was restored at Black Creek Pioneer Village in 1967 as a typical inn of the mid-nineteenth century. Lilacs, in the foreground, were a favorite shrub of most settlers to Upper Canada.

11

PREPARING THE LAND

The preparation of the land meant clearing the bush and chopping down giant-sized trees, with nothing more than an axe to do the job. Some settlers burned the trees down. Others girdled them by cutting a broad ring around the trunk, thus killing the tree by preventing the flow of sap. Either way, it was a slow laborious task that took years to accomplish.

John Langton, in letters published in 1883 under the title of *Early Days in Upper Canada*, tells us that it usually took a settler three years to clear about thirty acres. Making allowances for stumps, he was left with about twenty acres for planting crops that could produce food. For this reason, the house or yard gardens, planted close to the cabins, were of vital importance for survival. Here the women planted the roots and seeds of vegetables, herbs, and flowers and a few useful shrubs in the roughly cleared earth. They were not interested in planned gardens in those first hard years.

The real urgency was for food to carry the settler through the harsh winters. So the first plants and seeds to be sown were those that provided food.

EARLY GARDEN PLANS

Research has not revealed any plans of flower beds around the earliest dwellings, but it does indicate that most women made small informal beds where flowers and vegetables were grown together, arranged only with convenience in mind. These gardens were fenced when located near roads or in neighbourhoods where animals roamed, and the best fences were quickly made from freshly cut osiers stuck in the ground and twisted to form a close, thick wall, an excellent background for roses and low shrubs. Such gardens were the special domain of wo-

Above: Fifteen Years after Settlement. *From "Three Views in the Life of a Canadian Farmer." Improvements have been made to dwelling and outbuildings. A large area of cleared land is under cultivation. Farm areas and gardens are fenced with split logs. Horses are drawing a hayrack, replacing the earlier oxen.*

Public Archives of Canada, Ottawa

Right: Clearing large stones from fields and gardens was a back-breaking job. This stoning machine was used to lift and transport them to fence lines.

Below: "The Retreat," Home of Lieut. Col. John Johnson C.B., Township of Dunn, Ontario. *This water colour dated 1847 is by Col. Johnson's son, the Rev. William Arthur Johnson, founder of Trinity College School. The painting shows the kitchen garden at the front of the house, the orchard on the right, and trees and shrubs around the grounds. The gardens on the left are probably herb and decorative flower gardens. Note also the various kinds of fences and hedges.*

Metropolitan Toronto Central Library

STUMP MACHINE.

As this is the season in which farmers have a little time to spare for the purpose of removing those unsightly objects which deface the appearance and diminish the value of so many farms in Canada, vulgarly call'd *stumps*, we present them with a Cut of a recently invented Machine for dislodging these gentry from their time-honoured residence. It requires little description, as it explains itself. It is simply a long wooden screw, at the upper end of which is a nut, to which a lever is fixed for turning it. Without the frame, which any one can make for himself, the Machine can be had for about $25 or $30. It is warranted to pull up the largest stump. Mr. Edmundson, of this city, informs us that he will in two or three days have them for Sale.

Above left: From "The Canadian Farmer" newspaper, Toronto, August 28, 1847.

Metropolitan Toronto Central Library

Above: The pioneer often had to make his own simple wooden implements. The harvest rake, four-tined fork, and garden hoe are good examples.

Below: Gay zinnias against a picket fence at Black Creek Pioneer Village. As settlers prospered, lawns, flowers and ornamental shrubs occupied the space at the front of the house known as the parlour garden.

men and were treasured not only because they provided beauty and food but because they provided a pastime to relieve their loneliness. The women often exchanged seeds at social gatherings, and plants and seeds were some of the most welcome gifts one could bring home when returning from a visit. Included among the popular annuals of that day are some flowers unknown today.

All flowers, shrubs, and vines were grown informally in all the early gardens. Though the plants themselves were cultivated and maintained neatly, there was no attempt at design; each plant was simply tucked into the soil in the most convenient place.

While we do not know the exact size of the early gardens, nor how many plants were in a bed, we do know that the choice of what was to be grown was influenced by the personality, the nationality and the character of the gardeners. In later gardens, the size of the family income also was a factor. Gardens became larger as their owners prospered. The vegetable

14

Left: Tree roots presented a major problem for settlers as they cleared the land. It was an arduous task to get stumps out of the ground and move them to a fence row. However, once in place, they formed a solid pasture fence which kept the domestic animals in, and most of the wild animals out.

Below: All gardens were fenced to keep out stray animals. This is the Half Way House vegetable garden, which supplied enough produce to keep the inn stocked for a whole year.

garden was eventually relegated to the rear of the house. The flower beds, borders and flowering shrubs that remained at the front were called parlour gardens. There appears to have been tremendous rivalry among women to produce the most striking display. There were beds in the form and colours of the Union Jack and in the form of two-tiered wedding cakes; and others were filled with the latest varieties of roses from England.

ORCHARDS

In pioneer days trees were more often cut down than planted, since land had to be cleared for crops. With few exceptions only fruit trees were planted, fruit being one of the few delicacies available. Plum and apple trees and, in more temperate parts of the country, peach trees were important because settlers depended on the preserved and dried fruit to tide them over the long winter months. Wild fruits, berries, nuts, and other useful native plants were available for the gathering and helped to round out the winter food supply.

Left: Fences around a settler's home deteriorated very quickly, and shrubs and trees grew at will. Raspberries and crabapple trees are growing along this fence.

Below: In the Illustrated Atlas of Huron County, 1879, *Mrs. Elizabeth Southcombe's dwelling and farm are the picture of prosperity that came to some settlers following years of struggle in the wilderness. This shows a particularly fine example of the orchards which the settlers were eventually able to cultivate.*

Metropolitan Toronto Central Library

FARM RES. OF **ELIZABETH SOUTHCOMBE**, CON. 6, LOT 28, HULLETT TP. ONT

PLANTS INDOORS

Few early references to house plants have been found. With the limited space inside settlers' cabins, the lack of light indoors, and the extremes of temperature, it is doubtful if settlers in their first years would have bothered with house plants. They were more likely to have had a few dried branches of leaves or berries in a jug, and large bunches of herbs drying from the beams. Later records show that browallia, fuchsias, Jerusalem cherry, geraniums, and some fresh herbs in pots were carefully tended by the housewife.

Above: This plant is today the "Pelargonium Triste." Names of plants have been changed through the years as scientists learned more about them. Plant families have been divided into categories, and "Geranium" and "Pelargonium" are categories within the same family. From Jacques Cornut, Canadensium Plantarum Historia, Paris, 1635. University of Toronto Library

Right: Wild or Wood Geranium (Geranium maculatum). This is a water colour by pioneer Agnes Dunbar (Moodie) Chamberlin. It is also known as Spotted Geranium and Allum-root. The lovely blossoms are rose-coloured. It was once used to treat "indolent ulcers." University of Toronto Library

VEGETABLES

Fortunately for the settlers, the soil in most parts of the country was excellent for growing vegetables. This is confirmed by Catherine Parr Traill, who, in 1862, commented on "the rich black mould of the virgin soil."*

Potatoes, corn, pumpkins, squash, beans, peas, cabbage, turnips, and onions were among the staple foods in the early settlements. Turnips were important because they could be kept throughout the winter and could be enjoyed not only by the settler's family but also by his livestock. Here and there in the records of those days, however, one comes upon a complaint that turnips fed to cows gave the milk an unpleasant flavour and that pumpkins made better

Above: Wild Bergamot (Monarda didyma). *The blossom is a soft pink or pale lavender. Here again, the scientific name of the plant has changed since the seventeenth century. From Jacques Cornut,* Canadensium Plantarum Historia, *Paris, 1635.*

University of Toronto Library

*C. P. Traill, *The Canadian Emigrant Housekeeper's Guide*, Toronto, 1862.

Left: Flax, growing in the foreground of this garden is ready for harvesting. From it the settlers made linen.

Above: Pumpkins were grown by the Indians before the white man came. Settlers enjoyed the food they provided as did pigs and cows. Indians made bread and pudding from them. A decoction from the seeds was used as medicine among the settlers.

Below: Broom-Corn (Sorghum vulgare). Introduced by settlers, it was grown to make brooms and brushes and was food for cattle, horses and poultry. A decoction of the seed was a common home remedy.

M.T.R.C.A. Photo

food for cattle. Pigs, too, relished pumpkins and grew fat on them.

Early in the nineteenth century a wide variety of vegetable seeds was available for garden planting. Quetton St. George, a prominent merchant in York (Toronto), advertised in *The York Gazette* of February 20, 1808, that he had received garden seeds for red and white onions, green marrowfat peas, and blood-red beets. He offered for sale four varieties of cabbage seeds; three of cucumber seeds; melon and squash seeds; also early beans, cranberry beans and purple beans; as well as a good selection of herbs.

Nurseries flourished in many centres, competing vigorously with those in the American colonies. The Shakers in Lebanon, New York, carried on a thriving business in seeds and plants, advertising regularly in the Upper Canada newspapers and selling to customers directly or through local merchants.

20

Left: Daniel Stong's vegetable garden with his first home in the background. Tomatoes, carrots, beets, squash, and pumpkins were grown in quantity by the settlers.

In *The Patriot & Farmer's Monitor*, York, April 1833, J. W. Bent, a druggist, advertised that he was an agent for Shakers' seeds. Perhaps as a lure, the Shakers featured "Early Canada Corn Specially Fine" and a white-spined cucumber and a blood-red beet, listing both as Canadian in origin.

By this time, tomato seed, which is absent from earlier lists, was available. Beets came in three shades—yellow, white, and red. Red beets, however, were the most popular, no doubt because of the mistaken belief that red beets made red blood. It is interesting that the David Burpee seed house, one of the largest in the United States, introduced as a 1970 novelty a "new yellow beet," said to have originated in Canada.

"Large Cheese" was a popular variety of pumpkin. It is recorded that the Indians of North America were cultivating pumpkin before the arrival of the Spaniards. "Pumions"

were also great favourites of American colonists. Asparagus was commonly grown. There is a story of its being planted in Vaughan Township as a hedge between a garden and a dusty road.

Curiously, in the early seed lists, carrots were not highly regarded as food for humans. Perhaps the early varieties were hard and coarse; at any rate, one merchant commented that they were "for livestock only." By the 1860's, however, Catherine Parr Traill was urging women settlers to grow peas, parsnips, spinach, and salsify, in addition to those vegetables already in common use, and she included carrots. She writes that while sage, savoury, and peppermint were fairly common in settlers' gardens, basil, balm, and thyme seeds were "not easily got and sweet marjoram is not commonly met with." One vegetable from the early nineteenth-century nursery lists remains a mystery: the yellow turnip-radish.*

21

*This seed was sold in Canada as early as 1785; it is called a "yellow turnip-rooted radish" in the David Landreth & Company Catalogue, Philadelphia, 1836.

FRUIT

"...peach, apple and cherry trees grow on both sides of it, [Lundy's Lane] and bounteously project their boughs loaded with delightful fruit, over the fences, tempting the passengers to lighten them of part of their treasures."

—John Howison, *Sketches of Upper Canada*, Edinburgh, 1821.

In 1837, Charles Barnhart, proprietor of the Toronto Nursery on "Dundas Street, twelve miles from the City of Toronto" (the western boundary in those days was the present Bathurst Street), published a broadside offering for sale 85 varieties of apple trees. Few of them are cultivated today. Such varieties as Winter Codlin, Seek-No-Further, Bourassa, Wine Apple, Black Gilliflower, and Tewksbury Winter Blush seem to have disappeared. However, a few of the better varieties survived. We still have the Baldwin, Russet, Greening, Snow, and Fameuse; also the St. Lawrence, which was advertised by a New York nursery in 1850 as "that fine Canadian apple," which

Above: The Grape Vine. *In 1837 Anna Brownell Jameson journeyed to Richmond where she noted fine fruit growing which had been planted by the French a century earlier, especially grapes. From M. A. Burnett,* Plantae Utiliores, *London, 1840.*

Left: As a general rule, settlers removed all trees from the front part of their farms. However, before long, large fruit orchards were planted by most farmers. Some trees in Daniel Stong's apple orchard at Black Creek Pioneer Village have survived to the present day.

23

MENNONITE BERRY STURM

When the Mennonites came to Upper Canada they brought with them a simple wholesome tradition of food preparation that stemmed from their European beginnings. They relied on what their farms provided or on what grew wild in their surroundings.

Ingredients: 1 qt. berries (raspberries, blackberries, blueberries)
½ to ¾ cup white sugar
12 medium thick slices day-old bread (crusts off)
1 pint whole milk

1. Mash the fruit and add sugar.
2. Cut bread in small cubes and add to berries— allow to stand 10 min.
3. Add cold milk and serve.
4. This recipe makes 6 portions.

From *The Mennonite Community Cookbook* by Mary Emma Showalter. Published by Herald Press, Scottdale, Pa. Copyright © 1957, 1960 by Mary Emma Showalter. Used by permission.

originated in Montreal around 1820, and had developed from the seeds of decayed apples which had been thrown on a refuse heap in the garden of Mr. Henry Schroden. The famous McIntosh Red apple, one of the best known in the world, was also a chance seedling transplanted to cultivation by John McIntosh in 1811, on his farm at Dundela, Dundas County, not far from Ottawa.

The Toronto Nursery also listed a choice of green, yellow, and purple Gage plum trees, but cherry and apple trees were the popular ones for garden planting. Although no peach trees are mentioned, we know that other nurseries carried them before 1837. Quetton St. George, according to an advertisement of 1808, had peach trees for sale, also "plumb," nectarine, apricot, pear, and quince trees.

Right: Bunchberry (Cornus canadensis). *A charming native member of the Dogwood family. In the early settlements it was used as a tonic. The Indian women made dye from the ripe berries. Those who appreciate its flavour most are the wild ducks that haunt the damp shady places where it grows.* Photo by Ken Strasser

24

In *Winter Studies and Summer Rambles in Canada*, Anna Brownell Jameson tells of a journey she made in July 1837 to the hamlet of Richmond, opposite Detroit, where she enjoyed some fine fruit: "When the French penetrated into the regions a century ago, they brought with them...some of their finest national fruits—plums, cherries, apples, pears of the best quality and excellent grapes too."

Raspberries, strawberries, gooseberries, and red, white, and black currants were garden favourites throughout the settlements of Upper Canada, even though Mrs. Traill says that the countryside teemed with many of these fruits growing wild. And, "...back of Kingston," she adds, "there is a large cranberry marsh of great extent."

Left: Partridgeberry (Mitchella repens). *White flowers grow in pairs at the end of the stems, later becoming edible berries prized by the Indians as a delicacy. The Indians taught the settlers the medicinal uses of the plant. The young leaves were sometimes used to make a tea substitute. This is another water colour by pioneer Agnes Chamberlin.*

University of Toronto Library

Below: Red Choke-Cherries (Prunus virginiana). *The choke-cherry attracted the attention of the early settlers who soon learned that it made a luscious jelly. Indians dried the fruit and after thorough pounding added it to pemmican.*

Photo by James L. Parker,
National Museum of Canada Collection

Above: Bog or Marsh Cranberry (Vaccinium macrocarpon). *The fruit of this northern cranberry was held in great esteem by the settlers who prized it for preserves and pie-fillings. Today it is utilized to make jellies, drinks, and mock-cherry pie. An Agnes Chamberlin water colour.*

Below: Apples were cored, sliced, and dried, so that they could be used in the winter for pies, cakes and applesauce. Apple slices were placed on the apple-dryer (foreground) which was hung from a beam.

25

TEA, COFFEE AND CHOCOLATE

"...if the mistress of the hotel has none of the Chinese plant (tea) she will send one of her children into the woods to gather parts of the evergreen hemlock, hickory or other nauseous vegetable, and having made an infusion of the herb brought in, will enquire of her astonished and shuddering guest, if the tea is sufficiently strong."

—John Howison, *Sketches of Upper Canada*, Edinburgh 1821.

Tea, coffee, and chocolate were not readily available in the backwoods of Upper Canada, but the resourceful settlers found a number of adequate substitutes. Fragrant balm or bee balm (Oswego tea) was popular. Sweet gale and sweet fern were said to make passable teas, but there was more enthusiasm for tea made from basswood blossoms, various mints, bog rosemary leaves, young leaves of wintergreen, dried flower heads of white clover, and chamomile. Sassafras tea, made from the flowers, and witch-hazel tea, sweetened with maple sugar, were also popular.

Sage tea was considered a first-class nightcap, soothing to the nerves. Some of its popularity may have been due to the old wives' tale that sage had the power to restore youth to a person who slept with it under his pillow. By drinking their sage the settlers may have thought that they would get faster results.

Sage has been grown in this part of the world for more than three centuries. There is a record

Above: The Common Dandelion, displaying seedballs.

Photo by G. Marshall Bartman

27

Left: Barley, roasted over an open fire, was ground and used in place of coffee.

Below: Sassafras, Spice wood (Sassafras albidum). *White men and Indians enjoyed tea brewed from the young twigs and roots, which was sweetened with maple syrup. While it was important medically, the Indians did extensive trade in Sassafras bark. From Francois Andre Michaux,* The North American Sylva, *Phila., 1859.*   Metropolitan Toronto Central Library

of it in Newfoundland before 1620. Minnie Watson Kamm in *Old-Time Herbs for Northern Gardens* relates that a British sea captain, John Mason, brought eleven kinds of herb seeds for the Newfoundlanders to grow in their gardens; one of them was sage.

The settlers had fewer substitutes for coffee. The roasted grains of rye, the nut-like seeds of goose-grass, and the roots of dandelion and chickory, roasted and ground, made acceptable coffee. However, roasted barley was considered the best coffee substitute. Those who used it a century or so later during World War II will agree that it makes a mild, delicious drink. Coffee made from corn, a well-known Indian

beverage, was adopted by the settlers. Whole ears were dried and roasted on hot coals and then boiled, and the resulting brew was sweetened with maple sugar.

The young fruit of the basswood tree, when mashed, resembled chocolate in colour and aroma, but there is nothing in the records to show that the flavour aroused any enthusiasm as a substitute for chocolate.

For sweetening these various drinks, maple sugar, maple syrup, and sometimes honey were used. Peter Kalm, who visited Iroquois country in 1748-50, writes that the Indians told him that their people had never seen bees before the Europeans came.*

Left: Chicory, Blue Sailors (Cichorium intybus). *Upper Canada settlers cooked the young leaves to use as a potherb. The ground and roasted tap-roots were used as a substitute for coffee.*

Collection of Prof. J. E. Cruise, Botany Department, University of Toronto.

*Peter Kalm, *Peter Kalm's Travels in North America, 1770.* Dover Press edition, 1966.

Left: Mrs. Traill's Recipe For Making Coffee From Dandelion Roots: *"Prepare the root by washing thoroughly, but do not scrape off the outer brown skin . . . cut up in small pieces and dry by degrees until crisp enough to grind in the coffee mill. It is then used in the same way as the coffee-berry, with the addition of milk and sugar." From* Studies of Plant Life in Canada, *Ottawa, 1885.*

Below: Sugar Maple (Acer saccharum). *The Maple tree provided the settlers with sugar and syrup, and from the syrup they made vinegar. It gave them firewood that was second only to Hickory. Maple ashes yielded the best lye for soap-making and for pot and pearl ash that were readily salable. The timber was used by the wheelwright and wagon maker. Hard maple knots made useful beetles for splitting rails, and for driving posts and wedges. As the settler prospered he made furniture from this wood. From François André Michaux,* The North American Sylva, *Phila., 1859.*

Metropolitan Toronto Central Library

MEDICINE

"My Dear Mary,
    So you are likely to become a mother again...I shall now put down the articles for the syrup. If I can procure them I shall make you some.... Sarsaparilla, Hops, Burdock three or four roots, Prickly Ash Bark, Horehound, Cammamile, Tag Alder Bark, Gold Thread and Licquorice."

—Mrs Thomas Gibbs, South Oshawa, March 28, 1854, to her daughter Mary (Mrs W. S. Blackstock).*

Many women who settled in Upper Canada brought with them a store of medical folklore that had been passed by word of mouth from generation to generation. A number also brought books on home remedies that were produced mainly from plants.

It was the task of the women to grow and gather medicinal plants for poultices, salves, ointments, liniments, teas (tisanes), and other remedies that might be needed in time of sickness. Fortunately, by the time of the large migrations from Europe to Canada, many of the strange and often harsh ways of treating sickness had been given up in favour of the simpler remedies.

Originally, medicines made from plants may have been chosen by trial and error. The doctrine of signatures, which stated that nature

Above: Goldthread (Coptis groenlandica). *The intensely bitter juice of this plant was thought to be beneficial in treating Ague and was also considered a remedy for Thrush. Water colour by Agnes Chamberlin.* University of Toronto Library

Left: Laskay Emporium stocked cannisters full of dried herbs, which constituted a pioneer "pharmacy" of herbal remedies.

*The Gibbs Family letters, The University of Toronto Library. Used by permission.

had indicated the specific healing powers of plants through their appearance, may have had something to do with it. At any rate, plants said to promote the healing of broken bones, to relieve gangrene and gout, to reduce fevers, and to treat consumption and heart trouble, as well as an abundance of remedies to calm 'nerves', melancholia, and sadness, and to strengthen the memory, were set aside for medicinal purposes.

Roses, the kind that are considered old-fashioned today, were of such importance to the settlers that they were among the first things they planted. Leaves, petals, flowers, and hips were used to make medicine. A number of roses were grown from shoots brought from 'home'. Others grew wild, Upper Canada having a number of native roses. The

MRS. PALMER'S
VALUABLE RECEIPTS.

CONSTIPATION—ITS CURE.

2 oz. Senna. Simmer the strength out in two pints of water. Strain the juice to 1 lb. Prunes. Cook them till soft, with a handful of Sugar. At first take a table-spoonful of the Juice; after eat one Prune, fasting.

EMERODAL DISEASES, COMMONLY CALLED PILES.

Use a small candle rolled in the Golden Ointment: insert up the anus all night: wear this a few nights, and you will be well. Lubricate externally. Drink Fire Weed Tea or take 12 drops Fire Weed Oil daily for two or three days, and you will be well.

NERVOUS DISEASES IN THE HEAD.

Use a double handful of Salt to 1 quart of soft Water. When dissolved add 1 oz. Ammonia. Shake, and bathe the head freely.

TO STRENGTHEN THE NERVOUS SYSTEM.

1 Quart strong Slippery-Elm tea: 1 pint Black-Currant Wine: 1 oz. Tincture Iron. Dose—1 wineglass full three times a day.

BLACK SALVE FOR WEAK BACKS.

$\frac{3}{4}$ lb. Red Lead: 1 quart Linseed Oil: 1 pint Sweet Oil. Boil these till black and thick. Try it by dropping a drop in cold water—if it remain hard, it is done; if it spreads, still boil it. Spread it on wash leather. Apply to the parts. Wear it till it falls off; it will not irritate but strengthen: any enlargements or swellings it will reduce and strengthen. This for Chronic Rheumatism, put on leather round the parts is excellent.

WINDY SPASMS.

1 oz. Camphor put in 1 pint Rum. Take 1 table spoonful every 10 minutes till relieved.

LUNG DISEASE.

1 oz. Hoarhound; 1 oz. Camomile; 1 oz. Sassafras; 1 oz. Sarsaparilla; 1 oz. Black Cherry Bark; 1 oz. Comfrey Root; 1 oz. Alecapane. Boil these in 2 gallons of rain water, till you have one: strain clear: add 1 pint Honey; 1 quart Black Currant Wine. Dose—Two tablespoonfuls three times a day.

TONIC FOR THE LIVER.

Double handful of Hoarhound; the same of new Wheat Bran; boil in 2 gallons rain water down to one: strain clear: sweeten to your taste. When blood-warm, toast bread, cover it with Brewer's Yeast and drop in the centre. Cover warm and let it work all night. Bottle in jug. Dose—Half a tumbler full twice a day till better.

PILLS FOR LIVER.

Empty a Beef Gall in a pan; add $\frac{1}{4}$ lb. common Bar Soap; boil till thick. Add $\frac{1}{2}$ oz. Turkey Rhubarb, and let all mix. Form the pill with powder or flour. Take one or two a day till better.

COUGH OR COLD.

Take double handful of garden Sage. Put in a pan with 1 oz. Liquorice. Cover with best Vinegar and simmer the strength out. Keep it covered till done. Strain dry and sweeten with Honey to the form of syrup. Give a teaspoonful three times an hour till better.

ASTHMATICAL DISEASES, OR DEEP-SEATED COUGHS, WHOOPING COUGH, ETC.

Elecapane, Angelica, Comfry Root, Hoarhound Tops, Spikenard Root, Liquorice—each 1 oz. Bruse and chop fine. Boil then with $1\frac{1}{2}$ lbs. Honey, and 1 pint Black Currant Wine. When the strength is out, strain. Take one tablespoonful *hot*, three times an hour till relieved.

IMPERIAL DROPS, FOR GRAVEL AND KIDNEYS.

1 oz. Origanum, 1 oz. Oil of Hemlock, 1 oz. Sassafras, 1 oz. Oil Aniseed, 1 pint Alcohol. Dose—A teaspoonful three times a day.

RHEUMATISM, BRUISES, CUTS & WOUNDS.

$\frac{1}{2}$ gallon Alcohol, 8 oz. Green Wormwood, 4 oz. Arnica blows. Put these together and let them stand for a week. Rub by the fire, will cure. To add [illegible] any Angle worms purged into an oil and put with the above, is excellent.

GRAVEL CAN BE CURED WITH WILD LETTUCE.

$\frac{1}{4}$ lb. will make a quart of strong tea. Drink a teacupful twice a day. Two days will cure. Burdock, Nettles, Wild Rush—either of these made into a tea is good. Drink often of either.

TO TAKE FROST OUT OF THE FEET, AND TO STAY ITCHING.

Take goose manure and lard. Mix and apply to the parts.

FOR CROUP.

Take a few Hollyhock Blows. Boil into a strong tea. Apply the Blows round the neck, and wet every 10 minutes till better. Give a tablespoonful to drink every 10 minutes, till the child pukes.

The Golden Ointment is sure relief. Apply as a plaster round the neck. Keep wet cold cloths over, often changing. Keep the feet very warm, and good evacuations. Diet low for two days. MUMPS can be cured by this application.

DIPTHERIA & PUTRID THROAT.

Apply the same externally. Take Yeast and Charcoal for a gargle very often. This will not fail. Have free evacuations, and keep the skin clean.

TO CLEANSE THE SCALP & BEAUTIFY THE HAIR.

Bottle of Lyon's Catharion, $\frac{1}{2}$ pint Bay Rum, $\frac{1}{2}$ pint Olive Oil. Mix and bathe the head freely.

NURSING OR CANKER SORE MOUTH.

Break the small end of an Egg, and let out the white; have Borax and Alum ground fine, a teaspoonful. Take out a pan of hot coals: set in the Egg Shell and stir in the Borax and Alum. Stir till it acquires the consistency of paste. Make a mop of sponge and wash the mouth very often with it. Swallow some, as the stomach will be affected.

SALT RHEUM.

Golden Ointment will cure if you apply it externally and take cathartics to cleanse the blood.

SCALD HEAD

Can be cured with 1 oz. Golden Ointment, and 3 drams Red Precipitate, mixed together. Take away the hair: rub with this twice a day; and each day wash the head with warm Castile Soap Suds. ITCH can be cured the same way. This is for external application.

FELONS.

Make a poultice by taking Blue Flag boiled with Flax seed. Apply round the parts till better.

TO CLEANSE THE SKIN FROM BLOTCHES.

Take a teaspoonful of Stillingia twice a day till better.

TO CLEANSE THE TEETH.

$\frac{1}{2}$ oz. Orris Powder; $\frac{1}{2}$ oz. pulverized Charcoal; $\frac{1}{2}$ oz. pure Whiting. Mix and rub the teeth with brush.

CATARRHS.

Use Golden Ointment up the nose—plenty of it. Put some on the nose: let it be all night: in the morning bathe the face and ears with cold water. Draw some up the nose and throw it back. You will clear the Tubernated Bones.

CEMENT TO MEND CHINA.

1 lb White Glue; $1\frac{1}{2}$ pint Rain Water; $\frac{1}{2}$ pint Alcohol; $\frac{1}{4}$ lb. dry White Lead; mix all these.

WASHING FLUID WILL WASH THE CLOTHES WITHOUT RUBBING.

1 pint Spirits Turpentine; 1 pint Alcohol; 2 oz. Agrimony; 1 oz. Camphor Gum. Make up half a tub of warm soap suds and two tablespoonfuls of the above Fluid; put in your Clothes; let them lay all night. In the morning you have only to boil and rinse.

FOR DEAFNESS.

Have the fat from the Kidneys of wild Rabbit; gridel it out and drop in two drops in each ear, each night; rub cotton batting to a point, dip it in the Immediate Relief, and put in the ear. Let it remain till better.

ERYSIPELAS.

To 1 pint Cider Vinegar made hot, and $\frac{1}{4}$ lb. Litharge. Let it just simmer till it unites together. Then add one third of Olive Oil. Rub the parts affected often. Physic the system.

WARTS

Can be killed by getting the Oil from Angle Worms, and wetting the Warts with the Oil often.

SHAMPOOING MIXTURE FOR THE HAIR.

Take 1 pint of soft water; 1 oz Sal Soda; $\frac{1}{4}$ oz. Cream Tartar; bathe the head freely; wash it well from the Hair with soft water and soap. Every person should cleanse their head with this composition, once a week.

GREEN MOUNTAIN SALVE—FOR BURNS, RHEUMATISM, AND MANY DISEASES.

2 lbs. Rosin, $\frac{1}{4}$ lb. Burgundy Pitch, $\frac{1}{4}$ lb. Bees' Wax, $\frac{1}{4}$ lb. Mutton Tallow; melt them slowly.

When not too warm, add 1 oz. Oil of Hemlock, 1 oz. Balsam Fir, 1 oz. Oil Origanum, 1 oz. Oil Red Cedar, 1 oz. Venice Turpentine, 1 oz. Oil Wormwood, 1 oz. Verdigris.

The Verdigris must be finely pulverized and mixed with the Oils; then add as above and work all in cold water, as wax, till cool enough to roll. Rolls 5 inches long, $\frac{1}{2}$ of an inch in diameter, sell for 25 Cents a roll.

INFLAMED LIMBS.

1 oz. White Cedar Oil, 1 oz. Oil Hemlock, 1 oz. Oil Tansy, $\frac{1}{2}$ pint Alcohol. Rub the inflamed parts, and lay on rags wet with the same. The coolness will cure.

TO REGULATE GIRLS.

1 oz. Southern-Wood, 1 oz. Tansy, 1 oz. Catnip, 1 oz. Pennyroyal. Boil these in half a gallon rain water, till you have one quart. Drink a teacupful going to bed, while sitting over hot steam. Do this at the monthly period.

TO TAKE AWAY PAIN FROM BACK AND SIDE.

Spread plaster of Golden Ointment, and drop a few drops of the Immediate Relief over it. It will stay it in a few minutes. Wear a bandage 5 yards in length, $\frac{1}{4}$ yard wide; wet half of it; wind round the hips. Wear till better—keeping it wet. Rub well night and morning on the affected parts.

TO BRING ON EASY LABOR.

Have 5 or 6 Birth Roots; bruise them; put in 1 pint of Gin, and let stand a week. The last 6 weeks, take a tablespoonful a day. Eat or drink plenty of Slippery-Elm bark or tea. Rub the body very often with a damp towel.

LABOR.

To bring on tardy pains quick, get Peony Root; dry it, pulverize fine. Put a teaspoonful in a pint basin, and pour over slowly a pint of boiling water. Take half a tablespoonful every 10 minutes. When the woman perceives the pains are quick enough, desist taking any more.

CURE FOR WHOOPING COUGH.

1 Scruple Salt Tartar, and 10 grains Cochineal, finely powdered. Dissolve both in a tumbler of warm soft water. Sweeten well with loaf sugar. Dose—For an infant, $\frac{1}{4}$ part of a teaspoonful 4 times a day; for a child 3 or 4 years old, $\frac{1}{2}$ a teaspoonful 4 times a day; for an adult, 1 table spoonful 3 times a day.

Left: Very few doctors were available to serve the needs of the settlers during the first half of the nineteenth century. As a result, recipes for homemade medicines were vitally important to the whole family. "Mrs. Palmer's Valuable Receipts" lists a number of medicinal remedies which would have been used by many Ontario pioneers.

Below: After pioneer women had dried their herbs, they ground them for a variety of uses, especially for medicinal uses. They transferred the dried foliage from the stem to a mortar and ground it with a pestle. They sifted out the coarse material and ground the remainder to a fine consistency.

dried fruits were famine food for the Indians and were made into necklaces before trade beads were available.

Rose petals were gathered to make a soothing lotion for inflamed eyelids and another for a gargle for sore throats. Honey of roses was applied to ulcers, and a salve made from them was used to heal wounds. For migraine headaches, rose petal vinegar was used.

Widely diverse ailments, such as constipation and palsy, were treated with a rose conserve. Rose hip tea and syrup were prized for restoring vigour and muscle tone. Unwittingly, in rose hip tea and syrup, pioneer women struck gold, for, years later, scientists discovered that rose hips contain extraordinary amounts of vitamin C.

The shaggy grey-green clary sage had a corner in most pioneer gardens. Its glue-like juice was said to be excellent for extracting splinters. German settlers flavoured their beer with clary sage. Incidentally, these self-sufficient people brought with them to Upper Canada their skill for brewing beer and ale.

Garlic was a plant of importance because it was believed to have antiseptic properties in addition to its value as food and flavouring. The settlers had one extraordinary use for it, as a cure for baldness. The mashed garlic was thoroughly rubbed into bald heads.

Above: Maidenhair Fern (Adiantum pedatum). *An ancient book about ferns offers the information that "The Maidenhair Fern is especially potent in promoting the length of ladies' tresses." The settlers learned from the Indians how to make a decoction like "bitters" from the black fibrous roots.*

Photo by G. Marshall Bartman

Above: Puffballs (Lycoperdon gemmatum or Lycoperdon perlatum). *They are edible as long as they are pure-white inside and firm. The mature puffball is light brown in colour aud contains fine brown spores that fly out the top at the slightest touch. The spores have a healing quality and were used by Indian and settler on wounds and on the umbilicus of new-born infants.*

Photo by G. Marshall Bartman

Left: May-Apple, Mandrake (Podophyllum peltatum). *A single, nodding waxy flower, hidden under umbrella-like leaves, develops into a large, fleshy berry which is edible. The pioneers made a delicious preserve and jelly from them with sugar, lemon juice and ginger added. Leaves and roots are poisonous.*

Photo by G. Marshall Bartman

Garlic was also used to mask the flavour of meat that was not entirely fresh. Shredded garlic, mixed with honey, was a remedy for colds, coughs, asthma, and bronchitis and was also given to croupy hens.

Feverfew was the settlers' aspirin and, "bedewed with rum," was considered particularly good for a toothache. It is one of the oldtimers among medicinal plants and was one of the plants used in treating ague, which occasionally reached plague proportions in early days.

Many times when sickness struck the home of the settler, deep in the forest, he turned to

Melissa officinalis. Common Balm.

Far left: Hairy Puccoon (Lithospermum croceum). *Puccoon is an ordinary southern Ontario weed with yellow to orange blossoms. It is also the name of a plant dye used by the Indians for painting designs on their faces and bodies. The settlers preferred other plant sources to obtain this yellow. Water colour by Agnes Chamberlin.*

University of Toronto Library

Left: Lemon Balm, Sweet Balm (Melissa officinalis). *Today balm is still important as an ingredient in liqueurs, perfumes, and toilet waters. But it was known as a medicinal plant for centuries.*

Below: How to Make Rose Petal Vinegar: *Fill a glass bottle with fresh fragrant red rose petals. Pour white wine vinegar over them, filling the bottle. Stand bottle in the sun for two weeks; strain. This is delicious vinegar in a dressing for pear salad. The pioneers had many medicinal uses for this vinegar.*

his Indian friends for help. For centuries the Indians had used native plants to make their medicines. They passed on to the white man their belief in the red or wet-dog trillium to hasten delivery in childbirth. They showed the pioneers how to make laxatives from boneset, slippery elm, and May-apple; and poultices for swellings from the wild calla; and healing agents from puffballs and ground balsam root. The settlers learned how to put white or false hellebore on fresh wounds, blood-root on ulcers, and jewel weed on rashes and eczema. But the sweet flag was the Indian's cure-all. Florence McLaughlin relates in *The First Lady of Upper Canada* that on one occasion Molly Brant, sister of the Mohawk chief Joseph Brant and wife of Sir William Johnson, prescribed sweet flag for Governor Simcoe to relieve his cough.

It has been said that the women in the early settlements treated their sick with a mixture of home remedies and prayer. At least they met the challenge, and they carried on as well as they knew how and with great courage. It is

true that many of their patients recovered, but what part their remedies played in this cheering outcome is less certain. In many cases, their treatment probably had a psychological effect only.

Among the books of household medicine used in Upper Canada, the most enlightening are those that combine medical advice with moral homilies. The Reverend John Wesley, founder of Methodism, wrote such a book. Dated 1755, it is a pocket-sized manual with the title *Primitive Physic or an Easy Natural Way of*

Curing Most Diseases. Judging by the number of copies found in Ontario, it was once popular reading.

John Wesley reveals himself in his little book as a gentle, delightful man. Perhaps his sympathy for the sick grew out of his own affliction, palsy. He had great faith in plant remedies. "The use of sage," he wrote, "has fully answered my expectation; my hand is as steady as it was at fifteen."

He believed in sugar-coating the pill and was more than a trifle inconsistent. Under "rules for good health" he warns about the terrible consequences of drink, but under "instructions for making medicines," he condones a dash of wine or brandy as a finishing touch to most of his health-giving concoctions.

Many of the treatments he offered seem strange indeed, especially the one for ague, the disease most dreaded by the new settlers. It was essential to know an hour in advance when a "fit" was due, in order to give the

39

victim time to make a "plaister of yarrow and new milk" and wrap it around his wrist; or, as an alternative, to plunge into an icy bath, either outdoors or indoors, then dash into a well-warmed bed and sweat.

A fine example of sugar-coating was his medicine for colic, which consisted of "a little cardamom seed soaked in two pints of the best brandy, taken internally."

Dr. A. W. Chase, who had many followers in Upper Canada, was a different character from John Wesley, judging by his book, *Recipes and Information for Everybody.* He didn't believe in sugar-coating pills. His cure for ague was to swallow May-apple root with molasses, which "will sicken and vomit some, but will never need repeating." For earache he recommended hot onion poultices, and for bee stings, mashed clover blossoms—a remedy which he probably learned from the Indians. He advised summer savoury fomentations for bites of black flies and mosquitoes. His loathing for liquor prompted him to compose a poem ending on this high

Above: Cardinal Flower (Lobelia cardinalis). *A charming native plant that the Indians used to treat many ailments. The results so impressed a Mormon doctor that in 1824 he publicly declared the plant supernatural, and a nun advocated pouring a Lobelia brew into the sick until devils were driven out. The reaction was so violent that Lobelia lost its popularity. Water colour by Agnes Chamberlin.*

University of Toronto Library

42

Right: Day Lilies, Phlox, Purple Loosestrife and Bee-Balm growing in the gardens of Black Creek Pioneer Village. Hops on poles are against the fence.

note: "Gin slings have slewed more than slings of old." He disapproved of tobacco, urging women to cultivate mullein in their gardens and to encourage their husbands to use it for pipe-smoking.

Dr. John King's *Domestic Guide to Health* was apparently widely consulted in the early settlements. One suspects that he was a bit of a quack, but at least he was cheerful, and he was enthusiastic about plant cures for everything. He believed in caraway seed nibbles for sweetening the breath and catnip tea as an energy restorer; and he had faith in comfrey, chamomile, pyrethrum, flax, garlic, hops, geranium, lobelia, lily-of-the-valley, sage and horehound for treatment of various ailments. He prescribed the use of hemp to alleviate the pain of surgery as practised at that time in the colonies.

Germans who came to Upper Canada beginning in the late eighteenth century brought with them their distinctive plant lore, including a faith in plant medicines. They especially favoured betony, bugloss, feverfew, horehound,

Below, right: Formal gardens and borders had been developed in Ontario by the middle 1840's. In the background is the Daniel Flynn House, built in 1858.

Below, left: Yarrow (Achillea millefolium). This simple weed with white flowers has a reputation for healing that extends back at least to 1,000 B.C. The other names for it, such as woundwort and nosebleed, indicate its use. The Indians treated chills with a hot drink made from yarrow, first wrapping the patient in blankets and putting hot stones at his feet. Jacques Philippe Cornut, Canadensium Plantarum Historia, Paris, 1635.

Left, top: *Ground chicory roots were sold in a general store and used by the pioneer as a coffee substitute. Spices in the glass container were used for seasoning and preserving. The mortar and pestle came in handy for crushing herbs and spices.*

Left, centre: *A view of another area of the L-shaped herb garden at Black Creek.*

Left, bottom: *In early days it was the custom to dry herbs by tying them in bunches and suspending them from a beam in some warm, dry, airy place.*

licorice, rue, and tansy, and dried and stored large quantities of these for treatment of livestock and family. Many of the plants served a dual purpose. Although dill, caraway, cardamom, and fennel had medicinal uses, they were also grown to flavour foods. Madder was a remedy for dog bite and was an important dye plant. For whooping cough they made a tea from sunflower seeds, which, when parched and ground, made a flour substitute. They had a cure for warts that was simplicity itself: the application of a freshly cut side of an "Irish potato," one of the staple foods of all settlers. The British settlers believed implicitly in the orange-coloured juice of the celandine as a cure for warts.

Catherine Parr Traill, in the numerous editions of her book for prospective emigrants, urged women to take with them plenty of seeds of useful plants, especially marigolds. These she had found to be effective in treating cuts, burns, bruises, and gangrene. In her opinion, marigolds were the finest colouring matter for butter and cheese and one of the best yellow dyes for wool.

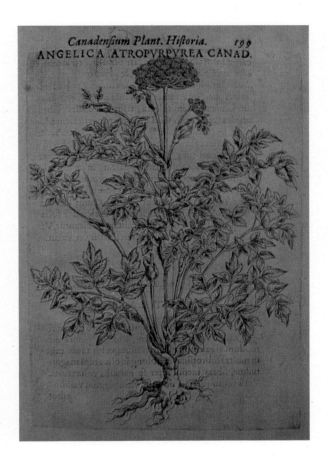

Left: Giant Sunflower (Helianthus giganteus). *Indians used sunflower seeds as an important source of food. They made bread from the slightly parched and ground seeds. They showed the white man how to boil the crushed seeds in water and skim the oil from the surface of the water to get a fine cooking oil.*

Above: Purple Angelica (Angelica atropurpurea). *The young roots and shoots of this native Angelica were candied in syrup and considered a fine treat. A strong hot tea made from the roots was used for colds, pneumonia, and rheumatism. It was one of the favourite dye plants, giving a clear yellow colour. From Jacques Cornut,* Canadensium Plantarum Historia, *Paris, 1635.*

University of Toronto Library

COOKING

Elizabeth Russell was a keen gardener and an experienced grower and user of herbs. She was a person of importance in Upper Canada as sister and hostess for her brother, the Receiver-General, who had a seat on the Legislative Councils of Upper Canada. Miss Russell's social position called for serving foods with a flair, but it is doubtful if the average settler's wife thought much about herbs in terms of cooking. She grew herbs in her garden for more important uses, such as medicines, but surely a number of the plants found their way into soups and stew pots. Great pots of beans and soup made from dried peas were the main-

Left: Before the period of the cook stove, baking was done in an iron pot beside the open fire. Thin batter was poured into a pan and set in a large iron pot to bake. Corn bread was one of the staple foods eaten by the settlers. Note also the bacon hung over the fire to be rendered.

Above: Garden Thyme (Thymus vulgaris). *There are many varieties of thyme, but the garden variety is a good one to start with for flavouring food. If planted in a sunny, well-drained spot and kept clipped, it will flourish for several years. Water colour by Agnes Chamberlin.* University of Toronto Library

stay of the early settlers, particularly during the winter. By adding summer or winter savoury to the soup, and adding sage, horseradish, and molasses (made from maple syrup) to the beans, they followed homeland traditions.

In the early days, Upper Canada abounded in game, and before many years had passed, pork and lamb, too, were in good supply on more prosperous farms. Garden sage, mint, garlic, dill, and thyme were probably used in the preparation of these foods.

Since the lakes and rivers teemed with fish, British settlers made good use of this food. Fennel or dill may have been added to the cooking water. German settlers used anise, poppy, and caraway seeds in breads and cakes and in beet and cabbage dishes. Coriander seeds flavoured many a pot of applesauce and many a pan of gingerbread. These herbs were used medicinally as well.

Tansy had an important role in the early households, as it contains a powerful bitter

There were a great many chores involved in preparing food for a hungry family. One necessary task for the housewife was baking the weekly supply of bread (left). Another was churning cream to make butter (centre). After the butter had formed, it was taken from the churn, washed, salted, and stored in a cool place. Beans were often strung and hung to dry, then shelled and stored away until needed for the soup pot (right).

juice which was used on fresh meat and fish in the hope of preserving them. How effective this measure was has not been recorded. To a limited extent tansy was used in cookery. Izaak Walton shows some enthusiasm for this herb as flavouring in *The Compleat Angler:* " . . . in the Spring the cooks made of them (minnows) excellent minnow-tansies, that is being fried with yolks of eggs, the flowers of cowslips, primrose and a little tansy; thus used they make a dainty dish of meat." Apple tansies as well as tansy omelets are mentioned in a number of mid-nineteenth-century English recipes. In Scotland, tansy was a popular

48

COSTMARY APPLE JELLY

Your favourite herb can be used instead of costmary, especially any member of the mint family.

1. Into a large preserving pot put generous handfuls of washed, fresh costmary leaves, harvested just before the flower buds open. Use only perfect young leaves and tender tips of branches.
2. Mash well with a potato masher.
3. Cut up 5 pounds of green juicy apples, and put them in the pot with the herbs.
4. Add water to ½ the depth of the apples and cover pot tightly.
5. Cook quickly until fruit is soft (20-30 minutes).
6. Place contents in jelly bag and let drip for 12 hours.
7. To one cup apple juice, add one tablespoon vinegar or lemon juice and ¾ cup sugar. Cook rapidly to jelly stage, that is, until two drops cling to spoon.
8. Pour into glasses and seal at once with melted paraffin.

CANDIED VIOLETS

Violets were used in the Upper Canada settlements chiefly as medicine. However, Miss Elizabeth Russell remarked that she put a handful of the blossoms in the water in which she washed her handkerchiefs, to give them a pleasing fragrance.

This recipe makes delicious candy and beautiful cake decorations too.

1. Cut the stems off clean fresh violet blossoms.
2. Spread them on waxed paper so that they do not touch.
3. Use a fine paint brush and coat every bit of each blossom with egg white, mixed with very little water.
4. Sprinkle generously with fine granulated sugar.
5. Allow the blossoms to dry.
6. Store in layers between sheets of waxed paper in an air-tight tin.

Below: Chives (Allium schoenoprasum). *In early days, flavourful chives were scattered among flowers and vegetables in the garden.*

flavouring in eel cookery. Tansy was brought to this country by early settlers for their gardens, but it soon escaped to overrun the countryside, to the delight of children, who call it "bitter buttons."

The rose-scented geranium was the pioneer woman's treasure, and on it she lavished great care. It held the place of honour in her window garden in winter, and it bloomed out-of-doors in a place of prominence during the summer. Its leaves were added to apple and quince jellies and were mixed with other herbs in sweet bags placed between folds of linen and clothing. Costmary (sweet Mary or Bible leaf) was another favourite. Delicate sponge cakes absorbed the fragrance of the leaves which had been placed in the bottom of the cake pan. It was also used to flavour junket and custard and, like the rose-scented geranium, was added to apple and quince jellies, fruit butter, and sweet bags. Costmary leaves are sometimes found in old Bibles where they were used as bookmarks —hence one of its common names.

MAKING DYE

"To die Madder Red on Woollen"

"To die one pound of goods, take three ounces alum, one ounce cream of Tartar, eight ounces Madder, half an ounce stone lime . . . fulled woollen cloth must be napped and sheared before it is died red then tenter it and lay the nap with a clean brush."*

—From *Cook Not Mad or Rational Cookery & Sundry Information of Importance to Housekeepers in General.*
Printed by James Macfarlane, Kingston, 1831.

In pioneer days, many farms had flocks of sheep which provided food, income, and wool for making clothing and household items, such as carpets, curtains, table covers, quilts, and blankets. Surviving examples tell us that our forefathers loved warm, bright colours, if not in their clothing, at least in their home furnishings. The dyes used to obtain these colours were made from plants and trees that were grown in the gardens or found in the fields, woods, and bogs.

One of the more important dye plants was woad, which gave a fine blue colour. In the beginning, the settlers brought seeds of woad from England and also from the American colonies, where it was extensively grown. By

Left: The housewife dyes her skeins of homespun wool in a brass pot over the open fire. Roots, barks, nuts and blossoms would produce various yellow, gold, and brown dyes.

Above: Yellow Bedstraw, Cheese Rennet (Galium verum). This plant was used to fill mattresses. The stems and leaves were used to curdle milk for cheese; the flowers provided dye to colour cheese and butter; the root produced a red dye.

*"Fulled" cloth is pre-shrunk cloth; to "tenter" cloth is to stretch it and hang it on a frame to dry.

51

Above: Dandelions in water in the dye pot over the fire.

Left: Bloodroot (Sanguinaria canadensis). *The juice produces red and orange dyes which Indian women used to colour moose hair and porcupine quills, and to stain baskets made of inner bark. These they sold to settlers. An Agnes Chamberlin water colour.*

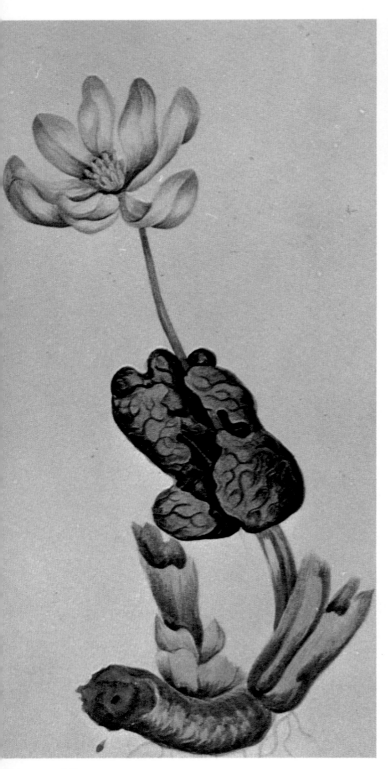

1830 woad seed was advertised for sale by a number of Upper Canada seed merchants. Our knowledge of woad, however, dates from ancient times. Julius Caesar landed on the shores of Britain and found the native people had dyed their bodies a ghastly blue, using this plant.

Yarns took on a beautiful green-gold shade when dyed with lily-of-the-valley; coreopsis and bittersweet produced a dye of a bright brownish orange. Balm blossoms gave a delicate pink, and dyer's madder, blood-root, puccoon (a wild member of the borage family), and the roots of bedstraw provided the warm reds and earth colours that were popular in loomed bedspreads, table covers, and hooked rugs.

For various shades of yellow and orange the women used sumac, marigolds, hollyhocks, blood-root onions, angelica, sweet gale, horse-

Below: Girls were taught to spin at an early age, and they soon became proficient. The fleece was sometimes dyed before it was carded and spun into yarn.

radish, and many other plants. Green butternut hulls gave a brown dye, as did the alder, but the richest brown came from the green hulls of the black walnut. Dyer's greenweed was grown in the American colonies long before the Revolution, and it is possible that it was brought to Upper Canada by the Loyalists.

Indian women showed the white women how to obtain soft, lasting colours from a number of wild berries. They made their dyes to colour moose hair and horsehair, and they taught the settlers how to obtain the same delicate shades in their wools. They made a brilliant red dye from blood-root, with which the braves painted their faces and bodies.

Dye plants were gathered as they came into season, and their buds, flowers, leaves, stalks, bark, and roots were used either fresh or dried.

LAWNS

"There is a plat of soft, verdant grass, directly in front of the house, which is skirted by a small grove, that stretches along by the side of the hill."

—C. P. Traill, *The Young Emigrants*, London, 1826.

There is much speculation as to whether or not grass lawns and plots surrounded the early homes in Upper Canada. And if they did, was the grass the same as that grown today? How was it kept in trim?

The early settlers had plots of rough grasses which were kept under control by the sickle or by sheep securely tethered to protect the garden. According to travellers, many of these areas about the farmhouses were cool, pleasant retreats in summer, where industrious housewives worked at their quilting frames or performed other duties while the children played.

In towns, and here and there in the countryside, there were what in those days were spoken of as lawns. It is not known how good they were or how smooth, but at least they

Left: Daniel Stong built his second house in 1832 using pine logs. The owner was already prosperous enough to afford the luxury of a lawn and a few decorative trees and shrubs.

Above: Common Evening Primrose (Oenothera biennis). *The root of this native plant is parsnip-like in appearance, and when cooked, it makes an acceptable vegetable. An Agnes Chamberlin water colour.* University of Toronto Library

55

served as a setting for lawn games or for summer visits and tea parties and after-dinner chats with friends.

Anna Jameson, in *Winter Studies and Summer Rambles in Canada*, describes a drive from Woodstock to London in the summer of 1837 in which she says: "... we passed the house of Colonel Light in a position of superlative natural beauty on a rising ground above the river [Thames]. A lawn, tolerably cleared, sloped down to the margin." On the same journey, Mrs. Jameson tells us she was the guest of Admiral Henry Vansittart and his sister in Blandford. She goes into ecstasies about the Admiral's house and its appointments and about the garden, but there is no mention of lawns.

But the diary of Miss Elizabeth Russell of York contains a number of references to her lawn and the many interesting gatherings that were held there. Miss Russell's lawn must have been made of turf or rough grass, because she arrived in York in 1792, well before the day of lawn mowers. In summertime, Miss Russell's garden, like those of all settlers, was an important social centre. In her diary she records

friends' visits to see her fine roses, to play a game of croquet, or to enjoy lawn bowling. She also makes frequent references to serving tea to her callers on the lawn.

On May 31, 1806, two ladies from Niagara visited her. They were taken to the lawn, "it being fine and warm." She writes, "I went into the house for my bonnet and when I returned I saw Mrs. M—— had got some white laylock in her hand and Miss C—— a yellow bachelor's button. These I supposed they had taken of themselves. Mary told me afterwards that Mrs. M—— tore the flower from the laylock and in her violence had broke another off. . . . afterwards Mrs. M—— asked if I had not the snowball tree. . . . I had one, but I took care not to lead them to the part of the garden where it was, lest it should be treated like the laylock, and they went in without seeing it. Gave them cake and wine."

What is certain is that when the settler had surmounted the hardships of the first years, his thoughts turned to a fine, comfortable home surrounded by smooth lawns and flower-filled beds, which were probably the status symbol of that day.

Left: "The Elms", Home of George Docker, J.P., Township of Dunn. *The Rev. William Arthur Johnson made this wash drawing in 1879. Worthy of note is the lawn mower being pushed by the woman. It surely was an early model, as there were none in existence before 1830.*

Metropolitan Toronto Central Library

Below: Residence of William Fowler 1879. Mr. Fowler was a livestock dealer, and his house and grounds were the epitome of style in Tuckersmith Township. The wrought iron fence had gates, hedges bordered the drive to the front door and ornamental trees grew on the lawns. From The Illustrated Historical Atlas of County Huron, 1879.

Metropolitan Toronto Central Library

IN ADDITION

"Some of the Most Probable Methods of Preventing Damage to Trees etc. by Sun-dry Insects

"Some vegetables are offensive to all insects; such as the elder, especially the dwarf kind, the onion, tansy and tobacco, except to the worm that preys upon that plant. The juice of these may therefore be applied, with effect, in repelling insects; and sometimes the plants themselves, while green, or when reduced to powder, particularly the latter, when made into snuff. Set an onion in the centre of a hill of cucumbers, squashes, melons, etc. and it will effectually keep off the yellow striped bug that preys upon these plants while young."

—From *Cook Not Mad, or Rational Cookery & Sundry Information of Importance to Housekeepers in General.*
Printed by James Macfarlane, Kingston, 1836.

The settlers had countless uses for plants beyond those mentioned here. One could recognize the gardens of the immigrant Scottish weavers·by the clumps of teasel that were certain to be seen growing in them. Its dried flower head, covered with firm, finely hooked bracts, was used to raise the nap on woollen cloth. The common Bouncing Bet was probably introduced into this country by the same craftsmen, as it was generally used in Europe as a spot remover. Also, many settlers relied on Bouncing Bet as a soap substitute. Today, soap made from Bouncing Bet has a beneficent effect on perishable natural fibres, restoring their elasticity and original colours.

The settlers found plants useful in dealing with fleas, ticks, mites, ants, and even bedbugs.

Left: Nearly every community had one artisan who earned his living by making brooms. He harvested enough broom-corn in the fall to last him until the following season. The broommaker often bartered his brooms for produce grown by other settlers.

Above: True or English Lavender (Lavendula vera). *Settlers from the British Isles cherished lavender, as it was beautiful and warmly fragrant. Hope chests and linen and clothes closets were perfumed with it. An Agnes Chamberlin water colour.*

University of Toronto Library

Farmers grew flax to make linen. The stalks were first soaked in water to soften the outer covering. Then they were crushed with a wooden brake (far left), before going to the scutcher (centre left), which removed the outer covering and centre core from the flax | *strands. The fibres were separated by combing the strands through the spikes of a hackle (centre, right). The cleaned fibres were then spun into linen thread (far right). Flax seeds were pressed to make linseed oil.*

The resin-scented sweet fern and the bitter tansy did an excellent job of chasing the pests somewhere else, though the deathblow for these pests was made of stronger stuff. Wild mint or water mint, "quick smell" as the Indians called it, did an excellent job as well.

Whatever the settlers required they had to produce themselves. They made boot-blacking from the nutgalls of oak trees and from elder bark. Writing ink was made with logwood chips added to nutgalls.

In the cosmetic department, hair pomade was made from lard (or beef marrow), apples, and rosewater, with a little alcohol to keep it from going rancid. Still another pomade was made of castor oil, thyme, and rosewater. Homemade lavender water and rosewater were usually on hand to soothe feverish foreheads.

The instructions for making "Admirable Hair Wash" include rosemary, maiden-hair fern, southernwood (old man), hazel bark, and other items. Chamomile flower rinse was popu-

Right, above: Roblin's Mill was built near Belleville in the 1840's and reconstructed at Black Creek Pioneer Village in 1968.

Below: The miller picked grooves in the millstone in order to produce better quality flour. Evergreen Press Photo

lar among blondes and redheads and was said to bring out the bright lights in the hair.

Most of the early household recipe books offer suggestions for tinting hair. For this purpose, sage leaves were roasted until almost black and then brewed like tea. An infusion of black walnut husks in spirits was more of a nuisance to prepare but produced better results.

Settlers who used snuff usually made their own. Since no two recipes are alike, perhaps they used whatever plants they could readily obtain. This old recipe sounds pleasant: " . . . rosemary, lily-of-the-valley, sweet marjoram, lavender flowers, dried and pounded to great fineness in a mortar of spices"; the instructions ended with " . . . it is agreeable and innocent snuff to be used for pleasure."

In brief, these are a few of the plants that

60

ROSE PETAL BEADS

Collect a 2-quart enamel cooking pot, a wooden spoon, an asbestos stove-mat, a smooth board, a bottle for a rolling pin, a selection of cutters (thimble, bottle caps, etc.), fine wire for stringing beads and a tube of oil paint.

1. Heat slowly while stirring constantly, 1 cup of fine salt, 1 heaping cup firmly packed rose petals, ½ cup water.
2. When mixture is a mish-mosh, colour it by stirring in oil paint, a drop or two at a time.
3. Return pot to heat, this time using the asbestos mat. Stir mixture vigorously until smooth, making the colour even or streaked, as you prefer.
4. Roll the mixture on the board to ¼ inch thickness, cut in circles with thimble or bottle cap and roll each piece in the palm of the hand until round or oval.
5. As each bead is completed, pierce and string on a wire. Suspend the wire in a dry, dark, airy place until the beads are dry, moving them occasionally to keep them from sticking together.
6. When completely dry, thread on coloured cord or dental floss.

PIONEER HAIR RINSES

Many pioneers made herbal rinses the same way they made tea. Here are a few variations used by early German settlers:

Sage Hair Rinse:
    Roast a large quantity of sage leaves in the oven until they are dark brown.
    Brew the leaves in water in the oven for two hours.

Chamomile Hair Rinse:
    Brew chamomile tea, using blossoms only.

Parsley or Mint Hair Rinse for Grey or Red Hair:
    Boil a handful of fresh greens in water for one-half hour.
    Strain the liquid.
    Cool it.

JUGLANS nigra
Black Walnut

QUERCUS alba
White Oak

JUGLANS squamosa
Shell Bark Hickory

our forefathers grew in their house plots or gathered in the nearby fields and woods. Many of the same plants grow today in the gardens of Black Creek Pioneer Village and in the meadows surrounding the houses; but though they have the same names as their ancestors, they are not the same. They have changed greatly in a century or more, and few of the original varieties remain. They have been hybridized over and over again and appear today in very different forms from the early ones.

Without these herbs, vegetables, fruits, and other plants and, of course, skill and knowledge to use them, pioneer life would have been a lot less pleasant. It would be close to the truth to say that, but for these plants, many of the settlers in Upper Canada would not have survived the first grim years in the New World.

Left: Black Walnut (Juglans nigra). *As fine houses replaced settlers' cabins, there was a demand for fine furniture. The beautifully grained and coloured black walnut was particularly suitable for the massive styles of the era. Black walnut tree bark, root bark and green nut hulls were extensively used in home-dyeing.* Centre: White Oak, Stave Oak (Quercus alba). *The wood of the white oak was used for making boats, staves for beer casks, naves of wagon wheels, railroad ties and beams. The outer bark provided tannin for tanning hides. Indian women made baskets from the inner bark.* Right: Shell Bark Hickory (Carya ovata). *A tough hard wood used to make whip and tool handles, spokes and spindles. From François André Michaux,* The North American Sylva, *Phila., 1859.*

Metropolitan Toronto Central Library

Opposite: The gardens in winter: Burwick House, the gentleman's dwelling at Black Creek Pioneer Village, which is furnished as it would have appeared in about 1844.

BIBLIOGRAPHY

Adams, J.—*Medicinal Plants and Their Cultivation in Canada*. (Dominion of Canada Department of Agriculture Bulletin 23 second series, Ottawa, 1915.)

Adrosko, Rita J.—*Natural Dyes in the United States*. (United States National Museum Bulletin Number 281, Smithsonian Institution Press, Washington, 1968.)

Anonymous—*Cook Not Mad*. (James Macfarlane, Kingston, Upper Canada, 1831.)

Anonymous—*The Backwoods of Canada: being the Letters from the Wife of an Emigrant Officer*. (London: M. A. Nattali, 23 Bedford Street, 1846.)

Barry, P.—*Barry's Fruit Garden List of American Fruit Origins*. (Orange Judd Company, 1891.)

Bartman, G. Marshall—*Canadian Wildflower Photographs*.

Beadle, D. W.—*The Canadian Fruit, Flower and Kitchen Gardener*. (James Campbell and Son, Toronto, 1872.)

Burnett, M. A.—*Plantae Utiliores*. (London: Whittaker and Co., Ave Maria Lane, 1840.)

Canada Board of Agricultural Transactions 1864-68—*Reports of Agricultural Fairs*. (Metropolitan Toronto Central Library, Baldwin Room.)

Chamberlin, Agnes Dunbar (Moodie)—*Canadian Wild Flowers*. Original water colours. (Department of Rare Books and Special Collections, University of Toronto Library.)

Chase, A.W., M. D.—*Dr. Chase's Recipes; and Information for Everybody*. (E. A. Taylor, Bookseller and Stationer, London, Ontario, 1873.)

Clarkson, Rosetta E.—*Green Enchantment*. (Macmillan Company of Canada, 1940.)

Cody, W. J.—*Ferns of the Ottawa District*. (Canada Department of Agriculture Publication 974, 1956.)

Cornut, Jacques Philippe (Cornuti)—*Canadensuim Plantarum Historia*. (Paris, 1635.)

Cunningham, G. C.—*Forest Flora of Canada*. (Forestry Branch Bulletin 121. Department of Northern Affairs and National Resources, Queen's Printer, Ottawa, 1958.)

de Gingins-Lassaraz, Baron Fred.—*Natural History of the Lavenders*. Translated from the French by Mary Wellman and Helen Batchelder. (New England Unit, Herb Society of America, Boston 1967.)

Dominion Forest Service—*Native Trees of Canada*. (4th edition, King's Printer, Ottawa, 1949.)

Fernald and Kinsey—*Edible Wild Plants of Eastern North America*. Revised edition by Reed C. Rollins. (President and Fellows of Harvard College—Harper and Row Inc., New York, 1943, 1958.)

Firth, Edith—*The Town of York, Volumes 1793-1815 and 1815-1834*. (Champlain Society for the Province of Ontario.)

Goldie, John—*Diary of a Journey Through Upper Canada, 1819*. Willman Spawn, editor.
—*Letters of John Goldie*
—*Descriptions of New and Rare Plants Discovered in Canada in 1819*. Communicated by Dr. Hooker, Willman Spawn, editor. (Edinburgh Philosophical Society.)

Gordon, Jean—*The Art of Cooking With Roses*. (Walker and Company, New York, 1968.)

Guillet, Edwin C.—*Early Life in Upper Canada*. (Ontario Publishing Company, Toronto, 1923.)

Gussow and Odell—*Mushrooms and Toadstools*. (Division of Botany, Dominion Experimental Farms, Ottawa, Canada.)

Howison, John—*Sketches of Upper Canada, Domestic, Local and Characteristic*. (Oliver and Boyd, Edinburgh; G. and W. B. Whittaker, London, 1821.)

Hulme, F. Edward—*Familiar Garden Flowers*. 2 volumes. (Cassell and Company, Ltd.)

Hunter, A. F.—*A History of Simcoe County*. 2 volumes. (The County Council, Barrie, Ontario, 1909.)

Jameson, Anna—*Winter Studies and Summer Rambles in Canada*. (Wiley and Putnam, New York, 1839. McClelland and Stewart, Toronto, 1923.)

Johnstone, Alex—*The Old Indian's Medicine*. (Saskatchewan Archaeology Newsletter No. 26, 1969.)

Judd and Speirs, editors—*A Naturalist's Guide to Ontario*. (F.O.N. Publication, University of Toronto Press.)

Kalm, Peter—*Travels in North America*. Adolf B. Benson, editor. From the revised English version of 1770, Volumes 1 and 2. (Dover Publications, 1966.)

Kamm, Minnie Watson—*Old Time Herbs for Northern Gardens*. (Little Brown, Boston, 1938.)

Kendrick, William—*New American Orchardist*. (Carter, Hendee and Co., Boston, 1833.)

Langton, Anne—*A Gentlewoman in Upper Canada*, H. H. Langton, editor. (Clarke Irwin & Co. Ltd., Toronto, 1950.)

Langton, John—*Early Days in Upper Canada, and Letters, 1833-37*. (Macmillan Company, 1926.)

Leechman, Douglas—*Vegetable Dyes from North American Plants*. (Southern Ontario Unit, Herb Society of America, University of Toronto Press, 1969.)

Leighton, Ann—*Look Down on the Plants*. ("Antiques" magazine, August, 1965.)

McLaughlin, Florence—*First Lady of Upper Canada*. (Burns and MacEachern, Toronto, 1968.)

Metropolitan Toronto Central Library, Baldwin Room:
Russell Family Papers
The Lossing Letters
Johnson water colours

Ministry of Agriculture, Fisheries and Food—*Herbs, Culinary and Medicinal*. Bulletin Number 76. (H.M. Stationery Office London, 1960.)

Montgomery, F. H.—*Plants from Sea to Sea*. (Ryerson Press, 1966.)

Montreal Agricultural and Horticultural Society—*Report, 1866*.

The Montreal Star, *Wildflowers of Canada*. 1893

Moodie, Susanna—*Roughing It in the Bush or Life in Canada*. (Richard Bentley, London, 1852, Publisher in Ordinary to Her Majesty.)

Murrell, Edwin—*Shrewsbury Roses*. Annual. (Portland Nurseries, Oteley Road, Shrewsbury, England.)

Ontario Archives, Toronto.
Newspapers and Periodicals:
"The York Gazette"
"The Patriot and Farmer's Monitor," York
"The Canadian Agriculturist Toronto," Canada West
"Upper Canada Gazette or American Oracle," Newark (Niagara)
"The Colonial Advocate"
"The Daily Evening Journal," St. Catharines

Pennsylvania-German Society
—*Plant Names, Plant Uses, Plant Lore, Volume 33, 1923*.
—*Early Kitchens, Volume XLVII*.

Plant Research Institute, *Billings List of Plants Collected in the City of Ottawa, 1866*. Reprinted from transactions of the Ottawa Natural History Society, 1867, with commentary by William G. Dore. (Canada Department of Agriculture, 1968.)

Preston, Richard A. editor—*Kingston Before the War of 1812*. (The Champlain Society for the Government of Ontario, University of Toronto Press, 1959.)

Public Archives of Canada, Ottawa.

Schetky, Etheljane McD., editor—*Dye Plants and Dyeing* (Brooklyn Botanic Gardens Handbook Volume 20, Number 3, 1964.)

Schraven, Joseph G.—*Modern and Antique Roses*. Annual. (Pickering Nurseries, Pickering, Ontario.)

The Western Reserve Historical Society, Cleveland, Ohio—*Shaker Bulletins, Broadsides, Garden Lists*.

Thomas, G. S.—*The Manual of Shrub Roses*. Annual. (Sunningdale Nurseries, Windelsham, Surrey, England.)

Sherk, M. G.—*Pen Pictures of Early Pioneer Life in Upper Canada*. (William Briggs, Toronto, 1905.)

Soper, James H.—*Ferns of Manitoulin Island* (National Museum of Canada, 1963.)

Spotten, Cosens and Ivey—*Wild Plants of Canada*, (Gage, Toronto, 1937.)

Stemler, Dorothy C.—*Old Roses of Yesterday and Today*. Annual (Will Tilletson's Roses, Brown's Valley Road, Watsonville, California, U.S.A.)

Traill, Catherine Parr
—*The Canadian Emigrant Housekeeper's Guide* (Toronto, 1862.)
—*Studies of Plant Life in Canada* (A. S. Woodburn, Ottawa, 1885.)
—*The Young Emigrants*. (Harvey and Darton, London, 1826.)
—*Canadian Crusoes, Tale of the Rice Lakes Plains*, (McClelland and Stewart, 1923.)
—*Canadian Wildflowers* (John Lovell, Montreal, 1868.)

Waugh, F. W.—*Iroquois Foods and Food Preparation*. Anthropological Series Number 12, Memoir 86 (Canada Department of Mines, Geological Survey, Ottawa, 1916.)

Wesley, John—*Primitive Physic or an Easy Natural Way of Curing Most Diseases* (London, England, 1760.)